ALIGNED ACTION

THE KEY TO CEO EFFECTIVENESS

RON WILDER

ISBN # 978-0-9835153-0-2

PUBLISHER
Aligned Action, Inc.
3434-135 Kildaire Farm Road, Suite 143
Cary, NC 27518

Printed in the United States of America

COVER DESIGN by Angela Hardison, SeeSaw Designs
COVER PHOTOGRAPHY by Bryan Rierson

To purchase quantities in bulk, contact the publisher directly.
Sign up for updates and download the audio companion to
this book at http://www.alignedaction.com/bookaudio

First Aligned Action Printing, 2011

CONTENTS

ACKNOWLEDGEMENTS

This book reflects the influence of many people who have shaped my life and career. I would like to express my gratitude in particular to several who were instrumental in the development and completion of this book: the incredible Anne Braudy, for everything she does to support my work in the world; my awesome editorial team, led by editor-in-chief (and wonderful wife) Hardin Engelhardt, along with Karen Taylor and Julie Lass, who helped shape the earliest drafts; my mentors and colleagues from R.B. Webber & Company, who taught me the fundamentals of business strategy, in particular Stephen Plume, Robert Lauridsen, Craig Knoche, David Ewing and Natalie Furman; Michael Klein, in memoriam, for the opportunity to work with him up close and personal; Blake Johnson, a great teacher and innovator; Frank Robinson, Jim Smith, Brian and Lou Raye Nichol, Dan Grandstaff, John Lucy, Kevin Fox, Rami Goldratt, Gerry Kendall, Jim Horan, Jim Schleckser, and Pam Boney for teaching me a great deal about my craft; Patti Gillenwater for providing a speaking platform for me on many occasions to develop and refine

i

these ideas; Cindy Dauss, Elizabeth Partin and Karen Mathre, for being constant sources of support, opportunity and encouragement; Richard Averitt, first a client and now a great friend and business partner in new ventures; Dawn Averitt Bridge, for being a tremendous source of inspiration; Steve Chandler, my coach, for teaching me the discipline of writing and holding me to account to get this book across the finish line; Master Michael Macario, along with all of my fellow students at the Apex Ki Do Kwan, for creating a very special home for me; my beloved brother Randy Wilder; and of course, "my girls" – Hardin, Lacy, and Amelia – you are the best.

To you, the reader.

You are the creator of the future.

WHAT DOES IT MEAN TO BE CEO?

"Merlin, what does it mean to be king?"
— KING ARTHUR TO MERLIN IN *Excalibur*

One of my favorite movies is *Excalibur*. Released in 1981, the movie recounts the legend of King Arthur, Merlin, the Knights of the Round Table, and the quest for the Holy Grail. Early in the movie, young Arthur draws the sword Excalibur from the stone. This act reveals Arthur as the destined king, as only the true king would be able to remove the sword.

Immediately upon realizing his destiny, what does young Arthur do? He panics. While the knights are taking sides and gearing up for a civil war, Arthur flees into the woods, chasing after the wizard Merlin. Terrified, he asks, "Merlin, what does it mean to be king?" During a long, sleepless night, Arthur confronts his fears about the task ahead. With Merlin's guidance, young Arthur comes to grips with what he must do. Then he gets to work unifying the knights and establishing the kingdom.

This scene has always been striking to me. How is it that the most famous king of legend, this man who is destined from birth to take up the sword Excalibur and unify the realm, doesn't have a clue about what he is supposed to do? Why isn't he born with all of the knowledge, skill, and courage to fulfill his destiny? Why does he actually have to figure it out as he goes along?

The role of CEO is similar to a king in this respect. No one arrives in the role fully equipped. People come to the role of CEO from many paths – some aspire to it, some are groomed for it, some jump into it, others are thrust into it. Regardless of your path, the way forward can become cloudy – yet you are expected to figure it out.

I recall a conversation with the CEO of a very successful, fast-growing, profitable company. We had been working together for several months and he had made great progress in advancing his strategic agenda. At one point in the meeting, he asked, "I'm curious – what do you think I should be working on right now?"

The employee can ask that question of a manager – but who does the CEO ask? Where does the direction come from? To ask this question shows courage – not weakness. It shows a courageous commitment to discern the best path forward. Even the best CEOs will at some point confront this question: "What should I be working on right now?" Those who take this question seriously – and genuinely seek to discern the answer – are the most successful and effective.

My promise to you is that this book will help you answer this question: "What should I be working on right now?" It will help you focus your time, your attention, and your energy on those few critical actions that will create sustainable high performance in your organization. By focusing on these actions, you will significantly improve your personal effectiveness, satisfaction, and impact. Through these actions, you will become a more effective CEO.

IN A NUTSHELL

This book reflects my experience working with CEOs for over fifteen years. I've watched them work, worked with them, advised and coached them. I've paid close attention to who gets results and who does not.

This book isn't about leadership personality or style – you can have a unique style that is all your own. Rather, this book is about effective action – where you focus, how you spend your time, what you actually do. There are only a few really essential things that effective executives must do – and only you can do them. There is a huge difference in outcomes between those who focus appropriately and those who do not.

I encourage you to spend time with the stories and concepts in this book. If your company is already successful, this book will help you identify new opportunities for growth. If your company is not as successful as you'd like, it will help you identify where to focus to fix your company. This book is designed to help you answer the question: "What should I be working on right now?"

Here's the short answer:

1. The purpose of the CEO is to create sustainable high performance. For you to be effective as CEO, your actions must achieve this purpose.

2. Sustainable high performance occurs only through the aligned action of every individual in the organization. Aligned action occurs when each person, across all functions, takes consistent action that supports and contributes to the success of the business.

3. For aligned action to occur, seven essentials are required. These seven essentials must be strong, clearly defined, and in sync with each other, so that the people in your organization know exactly where they fit and how to act to bring about success. If any one of the seven is weak, missing, undefined, or out of alignment with the others, the organization will not perform at its full potential. Ignore these at your peril, since left unaddressed, lack of alignment will cause chronic underperformance and may result in business or career failure.

4. *If* your purpose as CEO is to create sustainable high performance – *and* sustainable high performance occurs only through aligned action – *and* aligned action requires seven essentials – then your work as CEO must focus on continually building, strengthening, and systematically aligning these seven

essentials. This work is unique to you, the CEO. No one else in your organization can do it. Therefore you must be relentless and disciplined in focusing your time, energy, and intention on this work. When you focus your time, energy, and intention on creating aligned action, you serve your customers, shareholders, and employees in the highest way possible.

5. Knowing what to focus on is only the first step – but by itself is not sufficient to create aligned action. The work of the effective CEO requires a different skillset than you might imagine: mastery in engaging experts. Mastery in engaging experts requires a high level of self-mastery as you grow into a teacher, coach, and facilitative leader. When you master the engagement of experts, you ignite discretionary effort – where people go above and beyond what is required to accelerate results.

THE TRUE WORK OF THE CEO

Imagine this scenario: You've been trying to connect with someone for a few weeks to discuss a business issue. You've left multiple messages by voice mail and email but you have not received any response.

When you finally reach the person, he apologizes profusely. Before you can say anything, he says, "I'm so sorry. I've been meaning to call you back. It's just that I've been so *busy*."

I've been so *busy*. How often do you hear that?

How often do you say that?

Now imagine for a moment that instead of the word "busy" this person used a different word: "effective." He says, "I'm sorry I didn't get back to you, but I have to tell you that over these past couple of weeks I have been so effective."

We generally don't say that in normal conversation. The implication to the other person is that he is not a priority or a part of your plan. Saying I've been "busy" is socially acceptable.

But for you as the executive, the mindset distinction is critical. Are you busy or are you effective? What's the difference?

Busy can be defined as being "actively or fully engaged or occupied," but also can mean "overcrowded" or "cluttered." We all recognize people who are always busy. They generate a flurry of activity without real results.

Effective describes action that "produces an intended result" or "accomplishes a purpose."

What about you? Are you busy – or effective?

WHAT IS YOUR PURPOSE AS CEO?

As an executive it is very easy to get busy. The demands on your time and attention are numerous. Everyone wants a piece of you. You can easily get distracted and pulled in many different directions. How do you know that you are working on the right things? How do you know that you are being effective and not just busy?

Effective action must serve your purpose. So let's begin with defining your purpose as CEO.

The purpose of the CEO is to create sustainable high performance. High performance incorporates sales, profitability, and growth. Sustainability incorporates innovation, culture, and succession.

Boards of directors, whose primary role is to select a CEO, want a CEO who does both. A CEO who can create high performance that is also sustainable creates tremendous value for customers, employees, and shareholders.

With this clarity of purpose, you can now evaluate the effectiveness of your actions and choose what to do and not to do.

WILL THE ACTIONS YOU ARE ENGAGED IN AS CEO LEAD TO SUSTAINABLE HIGH PERFORMANCE?

Before you answer that question, I'd like you to take a moment to think about an employee in your organization. He could be a sales rep, customer service agent, warehouse supervisor, or a financial analyst. She could be the manager of your R&D lab, a software engineer, or your logistics director for Latin America. Do you have someone in mind?

Imagine that right now, just as you are beginning to read this book, this person is arriving at work. They set their coffee on the desk, sit down in their cubicle, fire up their computer, and begin to work. Now consider the following:

- Will the things this person does today and the manner in which he does them, support your business goals or not?

- How do you know?

- How does he know?

- If he is not doing things which support the business goals, what is he doing instead?

- If he is not doing the right things to support your strategy, is it because: 1) he doesn't know what to do; 2) he knows what to do but doesn't know how to do it; 3) he doesn't want to do it; or 4) he wants to do it but he is missing something that would enable him to do it?

- Given the competitive pressures you are facing, how much time do you have to create the right action?

- What will it take to close the gap between his current actions and the actions required for success?

As you consider these questions, can you see how the action of this person either *is* or *is not* supporting the goals for the business? There is no middle ground here, no kinda-sorta supporting actions. Either the action is consistent with the goals of the business or it is not.

SUSTAINABLE HIGH PERFORMANCE OCCURS ONLY THROUGH ALIGNED ACTION

Now extend your thinking from this one employee to all of the individuals in your organization: is every person working on the right things, in the right way, achieving the right results?

Sustainable high performance for your organization occurs through aligned action: when everyone in your organization is consistently working on the right things in the right way, achieving the right results.

Aligned action encompasses all of the behavior across every individual in your organization. It includes all of the decisions that people make (or do not make), the actions that they take (or do not take), and the manner in which they carry out these decisions and actions. It includes every interaction the people in your company have with customers, suppliers, and each other in the course of their day-to-day work.

Aligned action does not mean perfection, but *good* – in the sense that the actions are effective in achieving your purpose as a company. It does not mean that people have certainty or a crystal ball about the future, but that they make decisions and take appropriate risks. It does not mean that individuals are micro-managed in a command-and-control hierarchy. It does not mean that there are no gray areas, but that the tradeoffs of various options are well-considered and understood in line with the goals for the business.

SEVEN ESSENTIALS FOR ALIGNED ACTION

People genuinely want to succeed and contribute. Through this contribution, they create meaning in their lives beyond a paycheck. Unfortunately, the system in which they operate often prevents people from operating at their potential.

What is required to create the conditions for success? What needs to be in place to enable capable people with good intentions to perform? In other words, what does it take to create aligned action?

For aligned action to occur, seven essentials are required. These seven essentials must be strong, clearly defined, and in sync with each other so that the people in your organization know exactly where they fit and how to act to bring about success. If any one of the seven is weak, missing, undefined, or out of alignment with the others, the organization will not perform at its full potential.

As CEO, you have a unique and essential role in creating and sustaining the alignment of these seven elements. If you decide to go unconscious or avoid addressing one or more of these, you run the risk of serious mis-alignment. Left unaddressed, lack of alignment will cause chronic underperformance and may result in business or career failure.

I will state the seven essentials here as actions and briefly explain their impact on performance. To be effective, a CEO *must do* these seven essential practices. While they are numbered, each one is equally important and interdependent. You must engage in these repeatedly and continuously over time to create the aligned action that leads to sustainable high performance.

THE SEVEN ESSENTIALS FOR ALIGNED ACTION

Essential One: Create a Complete Definition of Success.
People know exactly what is important and why.

Essential Two: Connect with Your Customer.
People focus on creating and delivering what the customer truly values.

Essential Three: Build and Re-build Your Business Model.
People know how to direct their energy to build the business.

Essential Four: Focus on Flow.
People work effectively as core processes are aligned with the business model.

Essential Five: Build, Organize, and Coach the A-Team.
People perform as part of a team that is designed to win.

Essential Six: Create a Communications Cadence Around Performance.
People act with a clear understanding of where to focus and what to measure.

Essential Seven: Engage Every Individual.
People engage effectively with a clear understanding of how they fit and contribute to the organization's success.

THE TRUE WORK OF THE CEO

The seven essentials are criteria to help you determine if you are truly effective – or simply busy. As CEO, your work must focus on continually building, strengthening, and systematically aligning these seven essentials. When the right action isn't occurring, your job is to diagnose what's missing and to work on root cause solutions. When you are planning for growth, you must focus on all of these essentials in a holistic way.

Let me illustrate with a metaphor: your spine. The human spine is comprised of 33 vertebrae. When your spine is strong and aligned, your body is able to perform a variety of tasks. However, when your spine is weak, injured, or out of proper alignment, you can experience pain in various parts of the body. The pain can range from relatively minor to completely debilitating.

When you experience this kind of pain, you have four options:

1. Ignore the pain and hope it goes away.

2. Take a painkiller.

3. Seek a temporary adjustment from a chiropractor.

4. Develop the practices and habits to maintain the strength, flexibility, and resilience that enable you to perform at a high level over time.

Alignment in your business is similar to alignment in your spine. The seven essentials for aligned action are like vertebrae – you want them to be strong and aligned.

Whenever a business is not performing as you would expect, when you are experiencing some type of business-related pain, you can:

1. Ignore the problem and hope it goes away.

2. Take a painkiller – by firing someone or engaging in a wide variety of heroic, fire-fighting measures to save the project or sales for the quarter.

3. Initiate a temporary adjustment – like a reorganization or marketing campaign that creates the appearance of action and some temporary relief.

4. Create a powerful practice of focusing on the seven essentials for alignment.

The work of the CEO must focus on these seven essentials for alignment. Anyone can ignore the problem, and lots of managers can implement a quick fix. You must focus on the root causes of sustainable high performance.

The work of the CEO is unique to you. There are a very select few who can insist that the organization set high standards for performance and discipline. There is typically no one else who can insist that the organization confront major gaps in alignment. It takes courage, determination, and perseverance, but it is essential. Many people are depending on you.

When you are doing the true work of the CEO, you inject powerful energy into your organization. Confidence increases and performance improves. People see what you are doing. They can tell when you are avoiding the actions that will really make the organization strong. When you grow stronger and take action, the organization notices and performance shifts.

When you are effective, you are fulfilling your purpose as the CEO. When you focus your time, energy, and intention on creating aligned action, you serve your customers, shareholders, and employees in the highest way possible.

_____

The next seven chapters elaborate on each of the seven essentials of aligned action. As you read each chapter, consider *your company*. Within *your company*, is each essential strong, clearly defined, and in sync with the others? Make careful note of any areas in which one of the seven is weak, missing, undefined, or out of alignment with the others. This diagnosis will help you answer the question: "What should I be working on right now?"

ESSENTIAL 1:
CREATE A COMPLETE
DEFINITION OF SUCCESS

Creating and sustaining aligned action requires a complete definition of success. With a complete definition of success, people know what to focus on and what to ignore. Without a complete definition of success, people work aimlessly on the wrong things or worse, ignore aspects of success which turn out to be vitally important.

As CEO, you must continually facilitate the creation of this complete definition of success and declare this intention for your organization.

Let's look at one of the most frequently *misquoted* presidential speeches ever.

Have you ever heard of John F. Kennedy's speech in 1961 – the one in which he proclaimed that, by the end of the decade, America would send a man to the moon?

This speech is often quoted in historical retrospectives. I've heard it used many times in leadership seminars as an example of a powerful vision. Unfortunately, when it's quoted, the second part of Kennedy's vision is frequently left out. This omission is a huge mistake.

Here's the complete quote from JFK: "I believe that this nation should commit itself to achieving the goal before this decade is out of landing a man on the moon *and* returning him safely to the earth."

The *"and"* is pretty important, isn't it? Success is not merely getting a man to the moon, only to strand him there to die. A complete definition of success requires that we also must bring him home, safely.

Once you have a complete definition of success, you can then begin to identify what is required to achieve it. For example, starting with JFK's complete definition of success for the Apollo program, one could see how it triggers many essentials. First, you'll need a rocket design, a command module, and a lunar lander to get you to the moon. You'll need to recruit, train, and equip a corps of astronauts to carry out the mission. If you're going to get your men home safely, you have to figure out how to deal with atmospheric re-entry and landing on earth. To do all of these things, you need to coordinate the actions of thousands of people over a multi-year period to complete the project. You also will need a lot of money. Your complete definition of success, combined with these requirements, can help you calculate resource requirements.

So how do you create a complete definition of success? Use the "AND" exercise.

1. State your initial vision, whatever it may be. (Landing a man on the moon)

2. Add the word AND.

3. Fill in the blanks with what else is important. (Returning him safely to the earth)

4. Add the word AND.

5. Fill in the blanks (What else is vitally important?)

6. Repeat, as necessary, until you have exhausted all requirements of success. To make sure it is complete, ask yourself, "If we did accomplish this, what would be missing that we might regret?" Now add that to your definition.

7. Now review your list. Determine what is essential and what may be negotiable. Once you have defined the essential elements of success, you can begin to define the requirements.

Here's an example of a complete definition of success for a business:

1. Within four years from today, we will create a market-leading company in the _____ industry

2. AND generate revenues in excess of $X

3. AND generate profits in excess of $Y

4. AND invest $Z in future product development

5. AND expand our distribution globally

6. AND build a company culture that recruits, retains, and develops great people

7. AND maintain the highest standards of ethics and integrity.

If you get to four years out and you've only done part of this list, you've only been partially successful. If you neglect to specify important aspects of culture or values, you also risk succeeding only superficially and not being happy with how you played the game. The point is to be intentional and specific about everything that is important to you.

This exercise may seem demanding. It is. The complete definition for success is essential to building exactly the company you intend to build. Great leaders are demanding and offer no apology. You must set the standard. You must articulate a complete vision and definition of success. If you never specify it, how will you build it?

YOUR ROLE AS CEO IN CREATING A COMPLETE DEFINITION OF SUCCESS

Your role as the CEO is facilitating the creation of the complete definition of success for your organization. By doing so, you align and focus the energy of the organization. By declaring this intention, you become an organizing force that articulates the highest aspirations of your organization and says, "This is where we are going to go."

ESSENTIAL 2: CONNECT WITH YOUR CUSTOMER

Creating and sustaining aligned action requires that your company develop strong, deep, and trusted relationships with your customers. With a strong customer connection, people in all functions of the company can come together to make decisions that ultimately serve the customer. Without a strong customer connection, internal pressures dominate and innovation efforts are misdirected.

As CEO, you must continually insist on actions and personally conduct activities that deepen your organization's focus on and connection with your customer.

Peter Drucker wrote that "the purpose of a business is to create and keep a customer." So here's an experiment: select a handful of people from within your company and ask each one independently to describe your customer. How many different answers do you think you will get? Even if you get the same answer, probe further to see how well people understand the wants, needs, and values of your customer.

Aligning action across your organization to serve the customer must start with a deep and shared understanding of your customer. If you only have a surface understanding, you are unlikely to create a truly valuable customer relationship. If you do not have a shared understanding across your organization, you are likely to see behavior that is not aligned around delivering what the customer values.

Aligned action breaks down when your organization is missing a customer-focused mindset, a deep understanding of your customer's world, and a routine that strengthens and reinforces customer connection. As the CEO, you must continually reinforce a deep and shared understanding of the customer at all levels of the organization. You must go beyond the names of companies or titles of decision-makers. You must get to the core of your customer's reality – their environment, their economics, their pressures, their deepest desires and motivations. Understand how they make decisions, then teach and foster that understanding throughout your organization.

What follows are a few powerful and perhaps unconventional approaches to connect with your customer.

CREATE A 100% COMMISSION MINDSET

The most powerful way to connect with your customer is to create a 100% commission mindset throughout your organization. It is often so easy to get distracted by internal issues and forget the customer. The "100% Commission Mindset" focuses all of your energy on actions which serve the customer.

A few years ago I led a multi-day workshop for high-potential leaders at a global technology company. One evening, they held a reception to bring together the senior executives in the company. At one point in the evening, I found myself in a circle of people from different parts of the company – sales, marketing, human resources (HR), research and development (R&D), and finance.

The conversation turned to a topic of interest for everyone: compensation. The discussion centered on how each person's compensation was structured. I listened as the various formulas were discussed. The sales executive's compensation was about 60% fixed with 40% performance targets, while his team of direct reports had lower base compensation and higher commission potential. The marketing, HR, and R&D folks had much higher fixed compensation and lower variable compensation. After a few minutes, one person in the group turned to me and asked for my thoughts on the subject.

When I told the group, "I am on a 100% pure commission plan," the facial expressions of the people in the group changed dramatically, indicating shock and surprise. One person asked, "How do you do that?"

Well, here's how I do it: I am the sole owner and employee of my business. Every single dollar that comes into my company comes from my customers.

What does that mean?

1. No matter how good I am at what I do, if I don't sell it, I don't eat.

2. Every single cost in my business must be paid for out of customer revenue or the cash in my bank account. If I don't generate enough client revenue, then eventually I run out of cash.

3. I get as much unpaid vacation as I want.

By framing my compensation plan in this way, I have focused my business strategy squarely on the satisfaction of my clients.

I am not suggesting that you put everyone in your company on a 100% commission plan. There are many good reasons to structure compensation differently for different roles, different types of people, and different stages of the company. For most situations, pure commission sales plans create big problems in attracting talent and establishing the right strategic alignment.

However, this experience got me thinking about the impact of compensation structures on our mindset about customers. If most of your compensation is fixed, does it cause you to neglect the customer, because you are getting paid anyway? As companies grow and add different specialized roles, it is very easy for people to become disconnected from the end customer. What would it mean for your business if you got everyone in your organization to adopt a "100% commission mindset?"

Let's examine a few principles of the "100% Commission Mindset":

1. Everything we do ultimately must be paid for by our customers. Customers not only pay for products and services, but they pay our salaries and benefits. They pay for all of our vacation, sick leave, and perks – ranging from company parties to candy in the lobby.

2. If we want more money coming into our business, we need to create more value for our customers.

3. If we don't understand specifically what customers value, how can we sell and deliver it?

4. If we are frustrated with our current customers because they don't seem to value what we do, then we either aren't establishing that value or we need to find different customers.

5. If our customers do not value what we do, they will not pay us. They will go elsewhere and we will eventually go out of business.

6. If we have investors who are financing the company right now, it is because they expect that we will attract customers. Ultimately, the only way to pay them back is with revenue and operating cash flow from customers. So if we are foregoing revenue now to invest in the future, we'd better make sure that we are building something that customers will buy.

I have found that the concept of "100% Commission Mindset" has helped me in my business by creating incredible clarity of focus on the client, based on my own self-interest in survival and success. What would it mean to create this mindset inside your company?

GO DEEP INTO YOUR CUSTOMER'S WORLD

One challenge of connecting with the customer is that different people in the company have different perspectives on who the customer is and what the customer wants. You must create a shared view of the customer.

To understand how these different perceptions can hinder a company's success, consider the poem *"The Blindmen and the Elephant"* by John Godfrey Saxe. The poem is about six blind men who are trying to describe an elephant. As the blind men touch the elephant on different parts of its body, each concludes, separately and incorrectly, that the elephant is a wall, a snake, a spear, a tree, a fan, or a rope.

Many organizations have a similar problem, in which the company's various departments – sales, marketing, operations, R&D, finance, HR, or IT – each have different views of the customer because they interact with them in different ways or because they interact with different parts of the customer's ecosystem (discussed in the next section).

When customer clarity is lacking, innovation and improvement efforts are scattered and unfocused. Decisions become challenging and contentious. As the executive, you must continually go back to the customer and connect your organization to what your customer wants.

Go deep into your customer's world to truly understand how to best serve them. To create a more complete understanding, consider three elements of your customer's world:

1. The customer's ecosystem

2. The customer's solution tradeoffs

3. The customer's decision process

CREATE A SHARED VIEW OF YOUR CUSTOMER'S ECOSYSTEM

Today's economy is complex, global, and knowledge-driven. The end product or solution delivered to your customer often involves a complex and dynamic ecosystem of partners in your supply and distribution network. What do I mean by "customer ecosystem"? To understand this term, please take out your cell phone and consider a few questions:

- Who is your carrier? (Verizon, AT&T, Sprint, T-Mobile, other?)

- Who owns and runs the cell phone towers that provide your service? (It likely is not your carrier directly.)

- Who provides the equipment that runs the network? (Lucent, Cisco?)

- Who pays the bill for your monthly service fee? (You personally or your company?)

- Who manufactured the handset? (Nokia, RIM/Blackberry, Motorola, Apple, LG, Samsung, HTC, other?)

- Who created the operating system that runs on your phone? (Apple, Microsoft, Google Android, RIM/Blackberry, etc.?)

- How much did you pay for your phone?
  (Do you really think it was free?)

- Do you use applications or games on your phone?
  Who created them? Where did you buy them?

- What regulations and taxes apply to your cell phone?
  (Hint: there are a lot of them. Just look at your bill.)

As a cell-phone user, you are the end customer of a complex ecosystem. You benefit from and pay for, directly or indirectly, all of the mobility and functionality of your phone – and it is provided by dozens of different companies. These companies form an ecosystem, a complex web of companies who combine to deliver the ultimate product or service to the end customer.

A business ecosystem is much like a biological ecosystem. A biological ecosystem, like a rainforest, involves a complex, dynamic web of life, cooperating and competing for resources. A business ecosystem goes beyond the linear step-by-step value chain. It involves a complex web of firms who contribute to the value provided to the end customer.

Business ecosystems extend beyond cell phones and impact many aspects of daily life:

- Music: When you listen to MP3s on your iPod, you are participating in an ecosystem that involves artists, record labels, the iTunes store, the media player on your computer, and even *American Idol*, a show that has completely redefined how new artists are discovered and transformed into mega-stars.

- Financial services: Buying a home, refinancing a mortgage, applying for a credit card, using an ATM, exchanging coins at a Coinstar machine, using a debit card, getting insurance or financial advice, and investing in your 401k – all of these activities involve a complex web of companies that provide specialized parts of the solution.

- Enterprise software: If you use software in your business, you are participating in an ecosystem that involves hardware, operating systems, databases, middleware, and applications. Sometimes the software runs on your computers; other times it runs in a remote data center, referred to as "the cloud."

As CEO, you play a vital role in positioning your company within your ecosystem. To create aligned action, you must create a shared view and understanding within your company of who is in your ecosystem, how it works, and where you fit. Who is the ultimate end customer of the ecosystem? Who is your direct customer with whom you exchange money? How do you connect to and relate to other players in the ecosystem? Without this understanding, focusing your sales and product development efforts becomes very challenging.

CREATE A ROBUST FRAMEWORK FOR SOLUTIONS

If you've been in business for any length of time, you've no doubt encountered the concept of "solutions." Unfortunately, "solutions" is one of the most overhyped and misused concepts in all of business. Everyone, it seems, from information technology companies to pest exterminators wants to be a solutions provider. Management teams go away to offsite meetings and return to declare that henceforth they are in the "solutions" business. They think that simply declaring that the company is in in the business of providing "solutions" is the magic solution to their business problems.

A solution is a set of products and/or services that satisfy a customer's desire or solve a customer problem. The exact mix of products and services, and who provides them, is part of the puzzle that you must figure out. Here's a simple example. We recently redecorated our family room and wanted a flat-screen TV mounted on the wall and connected to a surround sound system. I purchased all of the products from a major electronics retailer. I could have installed the equipment myself, but I chose to pay for the installation services offered by the retailer. They sent out a crew to set up everything – everything, that is, except for the installation of an electrical outlet. For that piece, I had to call a licensed electrician. So as the customer, I still had to do the work to put together the entire solution.

Since the complete solution likely requires a mix of products and services from your company and others, you must insist on a thoughtful conversation about the customer's solution options and tradeoffs. In many companies, it is tempting to announce a solution without a clear definition of the problem you are supposedly solving. The real heavy lifting comes when you operationalize the solution and determine exactly what products and services will be delivered to the customer, by whom, and under what terms.

As the CEO, you must create a robust framework to have a conversation about solutions. At a high level, you want to guide a conversation that converges on four main questions:

1. What is the problem that the customer is really trying to solve?

2. What are their alternatives for how they could solve that problem?

3. How would our particular solution provide a better alternative?

4. What set of tradeoffs is a customer making that would cause them to prefer our solution at a particular point in time?

Frame the entire issue of solutions from the customer's perspective. The solution is for them, after all. As a basic example, consider how many times you have bought an item from a store, only to bring it home and discover that "batteries are not included" or "some assembly is required." You haven't really bought a full solution, have you? You still have work to do or components to acquire in order to have a complete solution.

Here are a couple of exercises you can do with your team as part of this discussion:

Step 1: Define the ultimate end result and then list all the elements required to achieve this result.

Remember the old saying that customers do not want a shovel, they want a hole? Start by figuring out what the customer's hole is – what is the ultimate end result that they are trying to achieve? Now brainstorm everything that the customer must have in place for the solution to work in operation.

Once you have gone through this list, go through it again. This time, you can conduct the dinner party exercise. If you've ever hosted a dinner party, you know the feeling when your guests are arriving and you realize that you forgot something. These last-minute things are like batteries that are not included. Update your list accordingly. Make sure you have a complete checklist of everything that will be required. Once you have this list, you can move to the next step.

Step 2: List all of your customer's options.

Once you have defined all of the elements of the customer's solution, you can go to the next step: defining all of the various options for how the customer might choose to buy the solution. Remember this is not what you are offering (yet); it is simply considering the various ways that customers buy.

It may be helpful to consider an acronym that defines three points along a spectrum of customer options:

DIY-WBIFY-WRIFY.

DIY: Do It Yourself. This solution is for the customer who, metaphorically speaking, wants to go to Home Depot, buy tools and materials, and build it themselves. Some do it for the fun of it, some to save money (at least in their minds), or others because they believe that what they want is not available commercially. If you are providing a solution for a DIY customer, you are often providing tools that they use themselves to build something.

WBIFY: We Build It For You. This solution is for the customer who wants a general contractor to build it for them – whether it is a house or a computer system. They basically want to purchase a complete solution, sometimes called "turnkey," and don't want to deal with the details of assembling and integrating all of the parts.

WRIFY: We Run It For You. This solution is for the customer that wants someone else to run the entire process on an ongoing basis, like the owner who hires a property management service. This company then maintains the property at an agreed service level and coordinates all of the required components.

Is it possible for one company to provide solutions along this entire spectrum? Yes, but it may require a very large organization to do so. IBM for example, sells hardware and software to customers who choose to do it themselves, provides professional services to build entire systems for customers, and also will contract with customers to operate entire portions of their information and business systems on their behalf.

In today's economy, there are numerous variations of these themes. It is useful to segment the various ways in which a customer might create a solution. A solution framework allows you to think about competition more broadly – it contains the full range of internal and external alternatives available to your customer. Your offerings and business model must be positioned within this context.

CREATE A SHARED VIEW OF YOUR CUSTOMER´S DECISION PROCESS

There is an expression in sales that companies don't buy, people do. So while creating the ecosystem view is essential to understanding what is going on in your customer's environment, the ecosystem view by itself is not sufficient. It is also essential to understand the internal decision-making process inside your customer's organization. Creating this view is essential to crafting your sales and marketing approach by clearly defining your customer's decision-making process.

Start by clearly defining the decision-making unit (DMU) inside your customer's business:

- Who is the user of your product, service, or solution?

- Who benefits from the output of your product?

- Who generates input into your product?

- Who is the economic buyer?

- Who controls the budget?

- Who are the influencers/recommenders?

- Who else might support or block a decision?

Getting clear on the different players inside your customer is the first step. Now think about how these players would work together (or sometimes in conflict) to make a decision about your product or service. Depending on the maturity of your product or service, the customer may or may not have a clearly defined decision-making process.

Often these questions are neglected or delegated to the sales function – yet truly understanding your customer requires understanding how they actually operate. When everyone in your organization understands this aspect, they can be much more effective in providing value to your customer.

YOUR ROLE AS CEO IN CONNECTING WITH THE CUSTOMER

In my experience, a high percentage of business problems originate from a lack of focus on or a disagreement about the customer. As CEO, you are in a unique position to address this issue and build customer connection into the heart of your company.

Sometimes you as CEO are part of the problem. The CEO is frequently smart, analytical, and visionary. Often the CEO carries around a picture of the complete ecosystem in his or her head. The CEO is able to synthesize what she learns in all of her varied interactions with the marketplace. Yet the functions within the company often only see a part of the picture. They see one part of the proverbial elephant and act accordingly.

As CEO, you can overcome this issue by deliberately creating context about your customer. Schedule time to bring your people together to create a shared view of your customer's ecosystem. Draw a picture of all of the players in the ecosystem. Show how products, services, money, and incentives flow to the various players. Look for where the revenue and profit flows from the end customer's perspective.

Create a shared view of your customer's solution options, tradeoffs, and decision process. Who is involved in making decisions? What is most important to them? Insist that your sales leaders and product leaders educate the rest of the company about the customer.

As CEO, you can create customer connection through creating a routine where the customer is the center of your interaction. Go meet with your customers. Bring people from the organization with you, not just the sales rep for the account. You can have your sales force set up the meetings, but be clear that you and others are attending as well and that the agenda is not about sales. You simply want to understand their world and look for ways to serve them better.

A word of caution: your organization will resist this routine at first. Your sales leaders will say that it detracts from real work. Your sales reps will complain about bringing extra people to meetings until they see how this creates better relationships and actually makes their jobs easier. Others will complain that you are slowing things down. Do it and don't apologize.

ESSENTIAL 3:
BUILD AND RE-BUILD
YOUR BUSINESS MODEL

Creating and sustaining aligned action requires that you continually build and re-build your business model. With a strong business model, people know what activities to engage in to build the business, what tradeoffs to consider when making decisions, and how to direct innovation and creative energy. Without a strong business model, people begin to worry about the future. Performance deteriorates in a downward spiral as the highest performers leave to pursue better opportunities.

As CEO, you must continually focus on the strength of your current business model while re-building your business model for the future.

What is a *business model*? In its simplest sense, a business model describes how a company makes money. It involves making something and selling something. In a broader sense, the business model tells a story that is supported by numbers. Joan Magretta's article "Why

Business Models Matter" (*Harvard Business Review*, May 2002) states, "When business models don't work, it's because they either fail the narrative test (the story doesn't make sense) or the numbers test (the P&L doesn't add up)."

How long will your current business model work until it comes under pressure from new technology, competition, or changing customer wants? What will it take for you to reinvent your business model to ensure profitable growth in the future? These are some of the most critical questions that you must urgently and continuously face as CEO.

To stress the urgency of this question for you, I'd like you to consider a brief question:

Where were you on September 7, 1998?

You may not remember that specific day or what you were doing. September 7, 1998, was actually Labor Day, so perhaps you were enjoying the last day of a three-day weekend before heading back to work or getting the kids started in a new school year.

While you may not remember that specific day, can you recall what you were doing at that point in your life? Where did you live? Were you working in the same field or industry? Did you work for the same company then as now?

By now you are probably wondering: what is the significance of September 7, 1998?

September 7, 1998, is the date that Google was founded as a company. Sergey Brin and Larry Page, the founders of

Google, had been working on the idea for a year or so while graduate students at Stanford University. Yet September 7, 1998 was the date that Google was formalized as a company.

Depending on your age, certain events take on a defining quality, in that they give us a sense that the world has changed in a significant way. Think about events like the moon landing, the fall of the Berlin Wall, the space shuttle Challenger disaster, or the assassination of JFK. Most people can tell you with vivid detail where they were and what they were doing as these events unfolded. The news of these events created instant awareness and reaction that something significant had changed in the world.

Looking back, the founding of Google *was* an event that changed the world. Yet unless you were close to the company – as a founder, lawyer, or venture capitalist, you would not even know about this event, much less have a reason to view this date as having much significance.

Consider, however, what has transpired since. At the time this book is being written, Google is just turning 12 years old as a company. In less than 12 years, Google has grown from revenues of $0 to over $23 billion. (Yes, that is billion, with a *b*.) They are perhaps the fastest growth story on record.

Google's story is not just about revenue growth. Google has become a verb. It is not just a company, but something we do multiple times per day. We "Google" people to learn about them on the Internet and to search out all kinds of information on every subject under the sun. If you have installed a Google toolbar in your Internet browser, think about how ingrained Google has become to your daily life at home and at work.

Google's impact has been so significant that all of the major technology companies are reevaluating their strategy for how to compete. Even the mighty Microsoft spent the first part of 2008 attempting to purchase Yahoo! so that they could better compete in the changing environment. Yahoo!, which once dominated the Internet, is now struggling to adapt to the Google-dominated world. In roughly the same time span, Google's fortunes rose while Yahoo!'s fell.

But it is not just the technology giants who are impacted by Google. Google is impacting everyone's business. Think about how you search for products or services. Where do you go first? Now think about how your customers, prospects, employees, and investors find out about your company. Google has made information instantly accessible, affecting every business.

What is behind Google's rise to power? Some would say that they developed an innovative technology for searching the Internet. True, but new technology by itself did not get Google where it is today.

Google's power lies in the power of its ***business model.***

Google's business model success comes from two combined innovations: a search method for locating web pages on the Internet combined with a revenue model based on pay-per-click advertising. The story works and the numbers work.

In the same 12-year period of Google's rise, we have seen numerous other examples of business model shifts across industries:

- The Apple iPod and iTunes music store have reshaped the music industry.

- Traditional newspapers continue to see their audiences and classified advertising revenue vanish as online alternatives for news (blogs) and advertising (e.g., Craigslist, eBay) have emerged.

- The network television model has changed dramatically due to developments such as reality TV shows (e.g., *Survivor, American Idol*), proliferation of cable channels, and digital video recorders like TiVo.

- Blockbuster and other traditional video rental businesses have faced the new threat posed by Netflix and Redbox, which have completely shifted the nature of video rental.

- The financial services industry continues to change dramatically in the aftermath of the dot-com bubble and housing bubble.

Yet Google's continued dominance is by no means assured. In just the past few years, Facebook has emerged and now has over 600 million users worldwide. Facebook and Google appear to be battling for dominance in the Internet. Who knows what type of company could emerge and displace them?

Consider two studies on the rate of change that companies must deal with today:

- In a 2004 cross-industry survey of senior executives conducted by Bain & Company, over 80% indicated that "the productive lives of their strategies were getting shorter" and over 70% said they expected to have "significant new competitors" within the next five years.

- By 2020, the average lifespan of a corporation on the S&P 500 index will shorten to 10 years, down from 50 years in the 1950's, as companies are created and destroyed more quickly. (Source: *Creative Destruction*, Richard Foster and Sarah Kaplan, 2001.)

This book was first published in 2011. The significance of specific examples most likely will have changed by the time you are reading it. That does not dilute the point of this section – it reinforces it.

As the Google story and cited studies suggest, no business is immune from change that will ultimately threaten the core business. Even good business models eventually come under attack from competition, new technology, or changes in customer preferences.

YOUR ROLE AS CEO IN BUILDING AND RE-BUILDING YOUR BUSINESS MODEL

Aligned action requires a strong business model. People must understand and have confidence in the overall business and understand where they fit. However, when your business model weakens due to changes in customers, technology, competition, or regulations, then aligned action can quickly begin to unravel. Just as a dog smells fear, your best people can sense when the business model is not working even before there is confirming data.

As CEO, you must focus on the strength and execution of your current business model *and* re-build your business model for the future. The challenge is that most of your time, money, energy, resources, and people are focused on executing your current business model. As CEO, you must **also focus your own time and energy to figure out the future business model.** What business will you be in a few years from now? The decisions you make or fail to make today will determine your position a few years out. Generally, only you are in a position to focus your organization on these issues.

CEOs who get too absorbed in the day-to-day activities of the current business may be successful for a period of time, but the long-term health and viability of the business suffers. The next chapters will help you get a good team in place and improve the execution of the current business – which frees up time and mind space to focus on the future.

ESSENTIAL 4:
FOCUS ON FLOW

Creating and sustaining aligned action requires core business processes that flow to generate profitable revenue growth. With a focus on flow, work gets done smoothly as customers, products, services, and cash move through your business. Without a focus on flow, profitable revenue growth is impossible as bottlenecks create obstacles to satisfying the customer and generating cash.

As CEO, you must continually focus on flow by aligning capacity and creating the right behaviors for daily execution. You must also create a culture of ongoing improvement that anticipates and alleviates constraints to growth.

ALIGN YOUR CAPACITY WITH YOUR PROMISES

At the core of your business model is a promise that you make to customers. The saying goes, it is wise to "under promise and over deliver." When you look at the overall structure of your business, you must make sure the right capacity is in place throughout the company to deliver on your promises.

When your capacity is not aligned, you may create short term results but sustainable high performance is unlikely. To illustrate, here's an example:

In the mid-1990s, America Online (AOL) was the dominant Internet Service Provider. They provided dial-up access from your home computer, via a modem, into their communications network. AOL was most famous for its e-mail program that announced "You've Got Mail!" when users logged into their accounts. Their business model was based on providing this network service to customers in return for a monthly fee.

During their most rapid growth phase, AOL's approach to acquiring new customers was to provide a free trial of one month's service. They blanketed the planet with promotional CDs which consumers could insert into their computers to initiate their free trial. These promotional CDs were everywhere – you could not open a magazine without finding a CD insert. CDs were sent via the mail and were commonly available at grocery store checkouts. Wherever a consumer might be, AOL CDs could be found. This marketing strategy led to its desired results: millions of new subscribers for AOL.

There was only one problem with this approach: the busy signal.

As millions of users signed up for the dial-up service, AOL subscribers began to encounter problems accessing the network. Imagine going to your computer, clicking on the AOL icon to log in to your account, and then waiting as your modem dialed into the network. You are anticipating the "You've Got Mail!" greeting and looking forward to reading and replying to your messages. Instead, you get a busy signal. You cannot get onto the network. So you try again and again until you succeed, after much frustration, or you fail and give up and come back at a later time. This problem created millions of angry customers, cancellations, and even lawsuits.

AOL could not deliver on their business model promises to their customers. While their marketing process delivered exceptional results by bringing new customers into the AOL network, their marketing process was out of alignment with the operational and customer support processes required to create a good customer experience. They simply grew faster than their capacity could support. A more balanced approach would have regulated the marketing investment and shipped out CDs only at a rate that the network capacity could support. In the days of the Internet land-grab, perhaps AOL management believed that as long as they could get customers, the network would eventually catch up. However, AOL's competition was catching up as other options for Internet access became available. AOL customers left and potential new customers selected other options.

As you grow your company, you'll want to carefully consider how the overall capacity of your company is structured and sized to deliver on your promises to customers and investors.

SHOW WHAT GOOD LOOKS LIKE

Aligned action requires daily behavior that is consistent with your business model. For example, when a Southwest Airlines gate agent executes procedures designed to quickly turn the plane at the gate, that behavior supports the entire activity system that represents Southwest's business model as the low-cost carrier.

However, the wrong behavior undermines a company's business model. As decisions and actions are embedded into your daily operations, it is essential that these behaviors are aligned with the business model you want to build.

When these behaviors are not aligned, the results are very costly. Consider some of these common issues:

- Have you ever sold a project that turned out to be a nightmare? What happened? Did you have the wrong customer or the wrong product?

- Have you ever "fought fires" to deliver a project that should not have been sold in the first place? What was the impact on the rest of the business during that time?

- Have you ever become enmeshed in hunting elephants? These are prospects who in theory could be great customers, but require so much effort to close that they undermine your other sales efforts? And if you do close them, they will overwhelm your ability to deliver, not just to them, but to all of your other customers as well?

- Have you ever spent time, money, and energy on marketing efforts, only to discover that you are attracting the wrong leads? Or that leads are wasting away due to lack of appropriate and timely follow-up by sales? Are your marketing, sales, and operations processes lined up so that you qualify, sell, and deliver the right product to the right customer?

- Are people in the company equipped and empowered to ask questions, to speak up, to raise concerns to make sure that the company is creating good business? Are they equipped to work with each other on a daily basis to support the business model?

If you don't like the answers to these questions, consider the impact on sales, profitability, customer satisfaction, employee satisfaction, and working capital.

The key to aligning daily behavior with your business model is to continually teach, demonstrate, and reinforce "What Good Looks Like (WGLL)." Repeatedly pointing out what people are doing wrong does not teach them how to fix it. Instead, show people what a good customer looks like.

Demonstrate a great sales call or customer support call. Model a highly collaborative decision that seeks input from all of the key people. Insist that what good looks like is communicated and demonstrated by your leaders in the organization.

CLEAR THE BOTTLENECKS TO PROFITABLE SALES

Let's do an experiment. Imagine I could hand you an order right now that would significantly increase the volume in your business? What would break?

I usually get one of three answers to this question:

1. Nothing would break. We could easily accommodate this order.

2. A specific process would break down, like logistics, manufacturing, customer support, or service delivery.

3. Forget increasing volume. Things are broken now!

This question, and your answer, reveals the primary constraint in your business. All systems have a constraint – a property that defines the total capacity of a system. Constraints can also be thought of as bottlenecks – the points where flow gets clogged up. At the point of constraint, whatever wants to move through the system must wait.

Some bottlenecks are temporary, like a traffic accident. The accident blocks the flow of traffic in one or more lanes.

Until the accident is cleared, cars pile up and flow slows as three lanes try to squeeze through one. Once the accident is cleared, normal flow can resume.

Some bottlenecks, however, are strategic in nature. They define the fundamental capacity of the system. Continuing the traffic example, think of a major bridge going into a city – the Bay Bridge in San Francisco or the George Washington Bridge in New York. Each bridge can only accommodate a certain rate of traffic and the toll plazas become a bottleneck that vehicles must squeeze through. Even if there are no accidents, there is a maximum limit of traffic that is eventually reached.

In a similar sense, your business is a system subject to bottlenecks. Understanding the primary constraints in your business system is essential to focusing your efforts to grow.

Let's go back to your answer to the question "What would break?" and identify your primary constraint.

If nothing would break, your constraint is external to the company – it is out in the market. You can handle more sales than you currently have without straining your current system. However, if something would break, then your constraint is internal.

To take this exercise a step further, imagine a volume knob controlling your business. Start gradually turning up the volume: 10%, 20%, 50%, 100%, etc. Where do you see things starting to break? These anticipated constraint points will help you plan for the growth of the business.

If you can turn up more volume now, then your constraint is in sales. You'll want to look at how you can generate more demand, more leads, and an improved ability to move customers through the sales process. You'll want to look within your sales process to find the bottlenecks to sales growth.

If you can't turn up the volume at all – if things are broken now, you'll want to identify the specific breaking points. Are they in operations, logistics, customer support, or service delivery? Sometimes they are in functions like finance, IT, or HR, as you start to outgrow your existing systems. If you have internal constraints, any efforts to grow sales will only lead to costly frustrations for your customer and employees, until you can alleviate these bottlenecks.

CREATE A CULTURE OF CONTINUOUS IMPROVEMENT

So what do you do when you've identified the constraint? Just throw more resources at the constraint, right? Not so fast. How you manage these constraints is critical to your success and can have dramatic implications for your profitability.

For example, consider an engineering firm, where a group of highly specialized engineers were approaching burnout. They were frequently working overtime or scrambling to complete work for their clients. In this case, the constraint was human, not a machine, as is sometimes the case – and the constraint was operating at full capacity.

The constraint was clearly identified, so the question now became, what to do about it? One idea was to hire additional engineers. Sounds appealing, but doing so would be a significant commitment. What else could be done?

By looking at the workflow that supported the engineers, it turned out that a lot of projects were getting to the engineers with incomplete information. The solution was to ensure that incoming projects contained all required information before an order would be accepted. This change was carefully communicated to customers and sales reps in such a way that they could see the benefit for them – their projects would be completed faster and on-time.

Another option was to raise prices. How much could rates be raised without losing business? After some discussion on figures ranging from 10% to 25%, they settled on 15%. A 15% price increase with no loss of customer volume meant that all of that money would flow to the bottom line. With the proceeds from this decision, the company hired support staff to help the engineers, rather than hiring more expensive engineers right away. The support staff further offloaded work from the engineers and allowed them to focus on the highest value engineering work. These actions created capacity for the engineering firm to take on much more work at higher fees, with a better quality of life for all of the people in the firm.

This story illustrates the application of one of the most powerful concepts for business improvement: *The Five Focusing Steps*. Eli Goldratt, author of *The Goal* and creator of the Theory of Constraints, outlines five steps to follow for ongoing improvement:

1. Identify the constraint.

2. Decide how to exploit the constraint. (*Exploit* means to use in the highest and best way, not in the sense of abuse.)

3. Subordinate everything else to #2. (*Subordinate* means that other policies support the priority of the constraint.)

4. Elevate the constraint. (*Elevate* means to raise the capacity of the constraint.)

5. Return to step 1. Do not allow inertia to take hold.

In the previous story, the engineers were identified as the constraint (step 1), but the idea of hiring more engineers would have jumped ahead from step 1 to step 4. There were many opportunities to better exploit the constraint (step 2), such as by raising prices and ensuring that orders were complete. Changing policies to insist on complete orders and adding support staff were ways of subordinating other actions to the constraint (step 3). If the company chooses to add engineers (step 4) at some point in the future, they will do so only when it is really required.

Sometimes it really does make sense to elevate the constraint in order to grow. This may mean significant investments in infrastructure and systems. For example, a maintenance services business found that their revenues were flat for three years in a row. They were profitable, but not growing. When they won new contracts, they would then struggle to deliver on them. They identified constraints in their financial systems which impacted their ability to manage more complicated customer contracts. After taking about six months to implement a new system and put in place more senior financial expertise, sales and operations were able to grow to the next level.

YOUR ROLE AS CEO IN FOCUSING ON FLOW

As CEO, you must continually focus on flow. When your business is not flowing, customers and employees both get frustrated and aligned action begins to break down.

A few actions you must take as you focus on flow:

- Align your capacity with your promises. Make sure you are not growing so fast that you create busy signals that frustrate your customers.

- Align behavior across the organization to create the right daily execution. Help people understand what good looks like in terms of decisions and actions that support the business model.

- Create a culture of ongoing improvement that identifies and manages constraints to growth.

- Finally, anticipate the constraints to growth and prepare your organization to make big leaps forward.

At some point, continued growth will require a step-function increase in capacity. These are major decisions with a big impact on the culture and operations of your company. While you can delegate the work of addressing current constraints, often it is you, as CEO, who must think ahead about where the next constraint points will be.

ESSENTIAL 5:
BUILD, ORGANIZE,
AND COACH THE A-TEAM

Creating and sustaining aligned action requires that you continually build, organize, and coach the A-team at all levels in your organization. A strong team, organized with the right structure and roles, and coached to perform, is capable of generating exceptional results. Without the right people, structure, or coaching, performance suffers and high performers leave to pursue better opportunities.

As CEO, you must continually build the strength and performance of your current team while shaping your team for the future.

BUILD THE TEAM THAT CAN WIN

A few years ago, I heard Mike Krzyzewski, coach of the Duke University men's basketball team, describe his experience as an assistant coach to the 1992 US Olympic "Dream Team." This team included the NBA's greatest players, including Larry Bird, Michael Jordan, and Magic Johnson. His biggest fear as a coach of this team was that even with all of the talent assembled, he might not be able to get them to play cohesively.

In the huddle with the Dream Team, he told them, "Not every team can win. But every team can lose." Coach K's point was that even with the best talent available, a team is still capable of losing unless they really play well together. While this team did in fact go on to win the gold, the 2004 Olympic Men's team did not. This later incarnation of the Dream Team, with a different roster of current NBA stars and a different coach, lost to Puerto Rico – in the first round.

Getting your team to work together effectively is certainly a critical part of your role as the leader. Yet the desire to focus on getting your current team working together can cause executives to avoid bigger questions and tougher decisions about the composition of the team itself.

My challenge to you is to carefully consider the first part of Coach K's quote: "Not every team can win." As the CEO, this concept is critical for you to understand, assess, and act on for two reasons.

First, your business is changing. As new technology, competition, and customer changes demand that your business model evolve, you must consider if your team is capable of winning. Second, your organization is changing, typically evolving through natural stages of development.

The players who were a good fit at one stage of growth may not be the best fit in a different stage. As CEO, you'll need to carefully consider these questions:

- What game are we really playing?

- What does winning mean to us?

- What does it take to win?

- Do we have a team that can win? Imagine your current team playing at its absolute best; will that team be capable of winning in the future?

- With the complete definition of success that we've now created, who on the team can grow along with us and who is simply not ready, willing, or able to make the leap to the next level?

- If you've recognized the need to change the structure or players on the team, what is holding you back from doing so?

ORGANIZE YOUR TEAM TO WIN

Creating aligned action requires that your team is well organized to win. Without the right structure, good people will struggle to work together effectively.

Defining your team is critical. In the broadest sense, your team is all of the people who are engaged in your mission, focused on achieving your complete definition of success.

In *Good to Great*, Jim Collins stresses the importance of getting the right people on the bus, in the right seats. Creating aligned action requires that you think carefully about the design of the bus itself – not just who is in which seat, but how the seats are configured.

Organizing your team to win requires that you think in three dimensions: Up-Down, In-Out, and Time-Complexity.

UP-DOWN

The up-down view requires an assessment of your organization's structure from top to bottom:

- Board of Directors
- CEO
- Direct reports to the CEO, whether you call this the senior executive team, the leadership team, or management team
- Directors and managers
- Supervisors
- Front-line associates

Consider each level of your organization. Is each level effective in doing the work that it needs to do? Do you have too many layers or missing layers? Does your organization create flow, or does it create bottlenecks?

IN-OUT

The in-out view requires that you think beyond the proverbial four walls of your company to consider your suppliers, ecosystem partners, and distribution channel.

When Henry Ford organized the Ford Motor Company in the early 1900's, he viewed his costs as beginning at the point at which raw ore was removed from the ground to the point at which the customer received the car. Based on this view, he built a completely vertically integrated company – even to the point where Ford owned railroads and mining companies.

Our world today is much different. In a globalized economy, anything and everything can and will be outsourced. Yet outsourcing is not the simple solution that the term suggests. Toyota, one of the most successful car companies today, invests a lot of time, money, and expertise in supplier development. Even though it does not own or control these companies, the company's results depend on their partners' effectiveness.

Consider a few recent examples of in-out decisions. Boeing made a strategic in-out decision to outsource production of major portions of its new long-haul jet, the 787 Dreamliner. But their suppliers were not equipped to manage a project of this scale, and this decision has resulted in very costly delays in bringing the new plane to market.

While most cell phone companies outsourced design of chips for their phones, Apple made the news by quietly recruiting a team of chip designers. They evidently determined that they wanted this expertise inside their company, not out, so they could further differentiate the iPhone from the competition.

Many mergers or acquisitions are premised on the idea of changing the in-out nature of the organization. For years, Pepsi was structured into two separate companies – the beverage company and the bottling company. In 2009, the beverage company decided to acquire the bottling company and bring those resources inside, believing that Pepsi would be better equipped to innovate and respond to changes in the beverage market.

The in-out view requires that you carefully consider your business model and the capabilities required to deliver on your promises. Getting this balance right is difficult, since outside suppliers have different ownership, incentives, and goals than you do. You must carefully consider the tradeoffs and risks associated with any possible configuration for your organization.

TIME-COMPLEXITY

The time-complexity view requires that you design your organization to do the right work based on its complexity over the appropriate *time horizon.*

We want our organization to work and to be capable of doing work. Yet many organizations suffer because they are not designed to reflect the nature of the work that they are intended to do.

Organizational psychologist Elliot Jacques pioneered a breakthrough in thinking in this area with his theory of "requisite organization." In other words, what is required in order for organizations to be able to do their work?

The key concept underpinning this theory considers the nature of work from two perspectives: cognitive complexity and time horizon.

1. How complex is the work itself, in terms of its cognitive content? For example, designing an airplane is much more complex intellectually than taking an order at a cash register.

2. Second, what is the time horizon of the work? In other words, how long will it take to observe the outcome of this work and determine if a person is effective in this work? For someone taking an order at a cash register, the time horizon can be measured in days. You can tell in a few days or less whether someone (with appropriate training) can be successful in this role. For a salesperson selling to businesses, or for a supervisor, it may take months or quarters to determine their effectiveness. For a CEO, you may not be able to observe their ultimate effectiveness for a decade or more, as the decisions

and actions they take today will determine their organization's profitability and strategic position years from now.

Jacques defined these levels of work as falling into different "strata." In the lower strata, the effectiveness of actions and decisions are observable in days or quarters at the most, while at the higher strata, it may take years to observe.

Jacques contends that people are managed best when their manager is one stratum above them in terms of their ability to handle complexity and time. This model also identifies two major organizational design decisions that can create all sorts of problems in communication and execution:

1. Skipping strata between reporting relationships (e.g. having a level I reporting to a level III.)

2. Having people with a higher strata capability reporting to a lower level (e.g. having a level IV reporting to a level III.)

Michael Raynor expands on this concept in *The Strategy Paradox* by pointing out how the focus of work shifts as you move up strata. At the lower strata, the business focus involves meeting commitments. Staff, supervisors, and managers are focused on delivering on promises to customers and achieving performance goals. In the upper strata, the focus is on creating strategic options. The CEO of a large company is not really concerned with day-to-day activities but rather with positioning the company for the future.

When you begin to really examine the work to be done in your organization to reach your complete definition of success, you'll find that this time-complexity view will help you organize people for success. Once you get the organization's structure corresponding to the complexity and time horizon of the work, and also matched up with people's capability, you will find that things work much better and aligned action results.

BUILD YOUR SUCCESSION PLAN FOR THE FUTURE

Organizing your team to win goes a long way – but if you do not have a way to grow leaders over time, you'll soon find that your organization's biggest constraint is talent.

To begin to assess your possible talent constraint, print out a copy of your current organizational chart. Now consider these questions for each role:

1. What is required from this role now?

2. What is required from this role over the next two years?

3. Is the person currently in this role performing well and also up to the challenge for the future?

4. If/when you require a successor, who in your organization is ready now for this role? Specific name?

5. If/when you require a successor, who in your organization will be ready in less than two years? Specific name?

Quite often this exercise is frightening. Certainly some companies will have a current succession plan, but when the business model is shifting rapidly and new capabilities are required, this exercise reveals a lot of empty spaces when you consider who is "ready now" and "ready in less than two years." If you find that this is the case for your organization, then getting good people in place is a critical priority.

Creating and maintaining a succession plan requires real work. Organizations resist the process because it generates tough questions about people, performance, and the future. The succession plan also falls into that category of "important, but not urgent," so it gets put on the back burner. Succession is never urgent until you have a critical vacancy.

The lack of a solid succession plan undermines aligned action because it reduces people's confidence in the future. When people see that you take succession seriously – that every role, including your own, requires a qualified, identified successor – they know that you are building a valuable organization for the long haul.

The lack of a succession plan also undermines your effectiveness as CEO. When your people see that you have a list of options, their own performance improves. If you have gaps in your succession plan that you tolerate, people will try to get away with bad behavior or underperform because they believe that you have no better options.

YOUR ROLE AS CEO IN BUILDING THE A-TEAM

While there are many opportunities to improve the effectiveness of your current team, any team will underperform if it is poorly structured, organized, or incentivized.

As CEO, you are in a unique position to improve the structure and alignment of your organization. You must continually build the strength and performance of your current team while shaping your team for the future by:

1. Creating the team that truly can win.

2. Organizing your team for success by looking up-down, in-out, and at time-complexity. Ensure the right incentives are in place to reward behavior.

3. Signaling your commitment to long term success and current performance through a rigorous succession plan.

ESSENTIAL 6:
CREATE A COMMUNICATIONS CADENCE AROUND PERFORMANCE

Creating and sustaining aligned action requires that you continually communicate your plan – and your performance against the plan. With a regular cadence, people know whether they are making progress and when to make adjustments. Without a clear plan, metrics, and milestones that are communicated regularly, people get frustrated by changing priorities and unclear expectations.

As CEO, you must continually communicate the plan and how you are performing against the plan. If this cadence is not a regular practice yet, here's how to start.

CREATE A ROADMAP WITH STRATEGIC MILESTONES

"Are we there yet?"

"Are you sure this is the right way? I think we missed a turn back there…"

If you've ever been driving with children or a spouse for an extended drive, you've probably heard those questions or concerns before.

Leading a company is similar to going on a long drive. Your fellow travelers, who are looking to you as the leader, will have lots of questions, both spoken and unspoken, about your journey. Not only do you want to carefully select your destination, but it helps to have a really good roadmap to guide you. You also must continually communicate with your passengers along the way.

A good roadmap for your business will include critical strategic milestones. These milestones show how you are progressing towards your complete definition of success. Strategic milestones also help you know what decisions you are likely to face at certain points along the way.

Good strategic milestones provide evidence that your business model is working. Some possibilities to consider include:

- New products shipped to the market
- Key customer references secured
- Cash flow turned positive
- Sales or channels established in key regions

Looking forward, what are the key milestones you anticipate as you create your desired future?

CREATE A REAL OPERATING PLAN

An operating plan is extremely helpful in creating aligned action throughout your company.

The operating plan is different from a business plan. The business plan is often prepared for a board of directors, bankers, or investors. It includes detailed discussion of customers, markets, competition, products, and financial projections.

An operating plan is more action oriented. It describes what you will accomplish, typically over a twelve month period. It includes measurable objectives and key initiatives. The operating plan specifies clear deadlines and assigns accountability to individuals for results.

A good operating plan is simple and clear. It improves communication across functions and creates accountability for performance. At the same time, the operating plan allows for flexibility in adapting to market conditions and opportunities.

In my experience, one of the most effective tools available for creating an operating plan that meets these criteria above is *The One Page Business Plan*. This system, created by Jim Horan, simplifies the operating plan to fit on one page by answering five key questions:

1. What are we building?

2. Why? (from the customer's perspective)

3. What will we measure?

4. How will we be successful?

5. What is the work to be done?

This approach to operational planning allows you to crystalize and document your thinking on many of the questions raised in this book.

Whatever format you choose to use, you must create accountability for results. Make sure that objectives are clear, well-defined, with names and dates assigned to each. A good operating plan serves as a powerful communication and accountability document to guide the operation of your company.

DESIGN THE RIGHT METRICS INTO YOUR DASHBOARD

Metrics designate what you want to measure along the way. Just as your car dashboard shows your speed and fuel level, it is important to have critical metrics available to you, the CEO, at a glance. What you measure is what improves.

There are a few fundamental measures you always have to consider:

1. Cash

2. Sales

3. Profits

4. Inventory or Working Capital

5. Customer satisfaction

6. Employee satisfaction

As you go through various milestones or as business conditions change, you may find that you need to monitor different metrics for a period of time. For example, I never really pay attention to the temperature gauge in my car; it almost always stays just below the mid-point during normal driving conditions. But one summer I was stuck in traffic driving through New York City during 100 degree heat, my car started to overheat, and the temperature gauge shot way up. I had to take immediate corrective action by opening windows and turning on the heat. Not fun, but better than stalling out on the approach to the George Washington Bridge. For the rest of the drive, I was watching the temperature gauge closely.

Business conditions can change as well, requiring a focus on particular metrics. The CEO of an industrial distributor monitored a core set of performance metrics, but left the more detailed financial metrics to his CFO. As the economy was heading into the downturn a few years ago, he wanted to have early warning signals to know if any of his customers were getting into trouble. He did not want to extend credit to customers who would become insolvent. So he moved a key metric for customer accounts receivables onto his dashboard. While his CFO still handled the operational aspects of receivables, the CEO was sending a signal to himself and the company that they needed to monitor the health of their customers closely.

By shifting key metrics onto your dashboard, you can really shift behavior in the company. A high tech CEO found that his leadership team focused nearly all of their time on the core product line, which represented almost all of their revenue. This made sense in the rapid growth phase of the company. However, success in the next phase required new products, and efforts to establish new products in the marketplace were not moving quickly enough. So the CEO added a metric to his dashboard that tracked the number of customer accounts running pilot projects with the new products. While the revenue was initially quite small, these pilot projects were critical to future revenue. Now he could look at this number every month and have deep conversations with his sales and product leaders on how to accelerate the success of these new products.

Are you tracking the right metrics? Do you have a good dashboard that provides performance data on what's important?

CONDUCT MONTHLY BUSINESS REVIEWS

Your roadmap, operating plan, and dashboard provide the guidance system for success. Now you must use it on a regular basis. Your communications cadence sets the rhythm for performance and decision making.

The most effective tool for establishing a powerful cadence for performance is the monthly business review (MBR). The MBR is a standing meeting with a specific agenda focused on tracking company performance. The meeting begins with an overview of company performance, followed by a brief, structured review of metrics and initiatives across the senior team. This process quickly gets everyone on the same page about the progress of the company. With this shared view of performance, you and your team can now have a robust discussion about issues and opportunities.

The MBR requires that you step out of day-to-day activities to assess your progress. With this regular rhythm in place, execution improves dramatically.

You can supplement the MBR process with other well-designed reviews that encourage strategic thinking and focus decisions at the right level. A quarterly business review (QBR) is similar in design, but allows you the opportunity to make more significant course corrections to address changes in the marketplace.

YOUR ROLE AS CEO IN CREATING A COMMUNICATIONS CADENCE AROUND PERFORMANCE

Aligned action breaks down because people don't know what's going on or what's important. As CEO, you must set the communication cadence for the company by insisting on regular and rigorous conversations about performance.

When you create regular space on the calendar, people know that performance really matters and that appropriate venues exist to make decisions. Remember that you are the person setting the agenda. If the right issues aren't being discussed, change the agenda.

Don't get bogged down in who might get offended or whose feelings might get hurt because they aren't invited to a particular meeting. Determine your agenda and then invite the right people who can most effectively contribute to the issue and decisions at hand. You are running a company, not planning a wedding.

ESSENTIAL 7:
ENGAGE EVERY INDIVIDUAL

Creating and sustaining aligned action requires every individual in your organization to engage in their work. With strong engagement, people understand how their role contributes to the success of the organization. Without strong engagement, people struggle to perform and this eventually creates a negative environment for performance.

As CEO, you must continually ensure the fit and engagement of every individual in your organization. Aligned action ultimately requires action at the individual level. You do what you do; I do what I do. When we are aligned, we get good results.

When people are truly engaged in their work, a powerful force is unleashed: the power of discretionary effort. Call it energy, enthusiasm, or love – it is what drives people to go above and beyond. When you can tap into this energy, your company becomes unstoppable.

CREATING THE CONDITIONS FOR SUCCESS

Here's where the rubber meets the road – engaging every individual in aligned action. Remember the individual you thought about at the beginning of the book? We examined how this person's behaviors, decisions, and actions either contribute to the success of the organization – or do not.

The first six essentials of aligned action all are focused on system-level issues that the CEO can uniquely address. As General Jim Mattis of the United States Marine Corps said, "When capable people with good intentions meet bad processes, bad processes win nine out of ten times." When you work through these first six essentials, you create the conditions for success.

Now it's time to engage everyone.

CONNECTING THE DOTS

It is not enough to simply create the conditions for success; you must clearly connect with individuals on where and how they fit. Consider this research:

- The number one factor determining employee productivity and execution is the degree to which they understand the connection of their role to the strategy of the company. (Source: Corporate Executive Board, 2007)

- Yet, in nearly half of organizations, employees do not understand the strategy of the company and senior executives and managers admit they *do not do an effective job of communicating the strategy.* (Source: International Association of Business Communicators, 2005)

While engagement and effectiveness depend on each person understanding how they fit, companies often do a poor job of making that connection. As CEO, you can ensure that all of your leaders and managers throughout the company do a better job of connecting the dots.

Imagine having a conversation with a current or potential employee about their role in the company. The first six essentials of aligned action create the framework for making this connection. You can frame your conversation as follows:

1. Here is what success means to us as company.

2. This is who our customer is. We understand what's important to them and act accordingly.

3. This is how our business model works now and in the future. Here's what we make, what we sell, and how we make money. These are our core promises to customers, employees, and shareholders.

4. These are the key processes that support that business model. We make sure they flow together on a daily basis.

5. Here's how our organization is designed.

6. Here's our plan of where we're going over time – the road map. Here's what we need to measure to keep track of our progress.

7. With those six essentials communicated, you can now have a conversation with this individual about where they fit: Here's where you fit – here's your specific role and responsibilities and how you have an impact on the organization and our success.

FOCUSING ON FIT

Now that you've laid the groundwork for engagement, there are a few other aspects of engagement that you cannot ignore.

A key first step: focus on fit – specifically how an individual fits into a role so they will be successful.

What is necessary for someone to be matched for success to a job? A good fit requires three components, like three sides of a triangle. If one is missing, the triangle collapses. They are all equally important.

- Skill: The person must have the skill to do the job.

- Capability: The person must have the capability to do the job.

- Values: The person must value the job.

The flip side of the triangle of Skills, Capability, and Value is "Don't Know, Can't Do, Don't Care." If someone is mismatched for a job, they are likely have one of these three issues: they don't know how to do it (a skills gap); they don't have the capability to do it (a physical, cognitive, or emotional gap); or they don't care or value the job (a motivation gap).

The real issue is whether a person is "matched" or "mismatched" to the requirements of job success.

When I was a little kid, I wanted to be a linebacker in the National Football League. I played football through elementary school and excelled at the position. I loved being just behind the defensive line, where I could see the field, watch the play develop, then quickly move to make a tackle or break up a pass.

Then something happened. Or rather, it didn't happen. Other kids on the team started to grow big and I grew to be, well, average. Linebackers in the NFL are typically six feet tall and weigh around 220 pounds. As I grew in junior high school, it became clear that I would be several inches too short and fifty pounds too light.

So if I showed up to try out for your team as a linebacker, would you characterize me as incompetent? Technically, yes. I am physically not capable of doing the requirements of the job. Yet the word "incompetent" has taken on a judgmental tone in our culture. Calling someone "incompetent" is done behind their back, because to say so to their face would be insulting. It also can cast judgment on their inherent worth as a human being.

However, such an assessment does not need to be viewed so negatively. Consider how gaps in each area can impact job performance.

- The skills gap: Does the person actually know how to do the job? Consider a computer programmer. This person loves to write code (they value and care about the job) and has a great knack for solving problems (they have analytical capability required of a programmer). However, their skills are in COBOL while the customer (either the project or their employer) requires Java. Unless this person can quickly close the skills gap, they will not be competitive for the job.

The skills gap is typically the easiest to address and is the focus of most training efforts. Unfortunately, the capability and values components are much harder to change.

- The capability gap: Does the person possess the cognitive, emotional, or physical capacity to do a particular job? In other words, given the right training and support, could they do the job? This gap is especially noticeable at key managerial transition points. A great programmer may not possess the raw capacity to be an architect, to think in terms of greater complexity or system design. A CEO might be quite effective managing a company at $20M in sales but be a disaster at $50M as the complexity of the business and the organization grows.

- The values gap: Does the person find inherent joy in the job that creates internal motivation? Finding the right values match is essential to high performance and happiness in a job. Consider a person in a customer service and operations role. This job requires exceptional attention to detail on a daily basis. Certain people thrive in these roles because they care deeply about each interaction and taking care of the customer. In another example, I knew of one HR leader who was exceptional in identifying and developing talent, yet her current job depended entirely on operational execution. She would spend her time on the areas of greater value to her and neglect the operational issues until they reached a breaking point. Then she would jump in and scramble to fix it. This was the problem – but she became perceived as incompetent in the organization. In fact she was merely mismatched between her gifts and the needs of the organization. Once she took action to shift into a better role for her, her performance and contribution improved dramatically.

When a person is mismatched, it is extremely costly to both the individual and to the organization. The individual is likely to be experiencing substantial stress because they are out of alignment with themselves, while the organization may be attempting to hide or cover for this person. One CEO I know calls "sanctioned incompetence" the great destroyer of company unity. I would change the term to "sanctioned mismatch." Once one comes out of denial and recognizes the mismatch, to let it continue is to sanction it. If you sanction a mismatch, you are sacrificing the entire organization to protect one person. In fact, you are also doing that person an injustice by having them do something they are unsuited. Looking back, most people regard getting redirected as a great gift, because they go on to find their true niche.

Engagement really increases when you have the right fit in all roles. So firing is not about the person; it is about the fit. People perform in jobs where they are aligned with their skills, gifts, and talents. If not, they might fake engagement for a while, but eventually their mismatch will be revealed through performance breakdowns, burnout, or other dissatisfaction.

CREATE POWERFUL AGREEMENTS

When you have a good fit, the next thing to do is create powerful and effective agreements with each individual.

Steve Chandler, the best-selling author and personal success coach, teaches a powerful concept called *expectations versus agreements*. Expectations in the workplace are ineffective and counterproductive. They invoke a parent-child psychology where the employee must try to live up to the expectations of the employer. In general, people do not like having to live up to the expectations of others.

Agreements are much more powerful and effective. Agreements are based on an adult-to-adult conversation about what each person commits to doing. People like to honor their agreements and keep their word. Agreements create much stronger personal accountability, which leads to greater organizational accountability.

CREATE CANDID COACHING CONVERSATIONS ABOUT PERFORMANCE

Good fit and good agreements by themselves will not produce sustainable results without consistent follow up. As tough as it may be, you must create candid conversations with people about their performance. When you do it well, people thrive.

We live in an ESPN culture. Founded in 1979, the all-sports channel has proven to be one of the most successful cable networks and a highly profitable one. It caters to an audience that loves sports. This same audience is also highly valued by advertisers.

On ESPN, performance of athletes is evaluated constantly. As ESPN expanded into multiple channels, their coverage of sports has expanded, and they now have lots of time to fill. What do they fill it with? Analysis. They analyze every aspect of the performance of players, coaches, and even owners. As an athlete, coach, or owner, your performance on and off the field is similarly subject to constant scrutiny and evaluation. You may not like the constant attention, but at least you always know where you stand.

Unfortunately, many business organizations go in the complete opposite direction about performance. Managers are fearful of giving open, honest, and constructive feedback on performance. As a result, employees do not know where they stand.

The best executives I have ever observed and worked with create a positive, candid, and constructive environment to discuss performance in real time. They look at the scoreboard: how are we doing? They look at the game film: where can we improve? How do we learn from mistakes? They look at themselves as well. When individuals understand that they will receive ongoing, real-time, and constructive input, they show up ready to play the game.

YOUR ROLE AS CEO IN ENGAGING EVERY INDIVIDUAL

As CEO, your role is to create the conditions for individual engagement throughout the company. You do this specifically by:

1. Working on the system-level issues that enable high performance, as described in essentials 1-6.

2. Connecting the dots between the business strategy and individual fit.

3. Ensuring that individuals are a good fit for their roles in terms of skills, capability, and values.

4. Creating robust agreements followed by candid, constructive conversations about performance.

The most critical, and often most difficult, aspect of this role is to make the tough decisions about people. When you have a mismatch, no one is served by prolonging the inevitable. Take a stand and make the people decisions that need to be made.

MAKING IT HAPPEN

This book began with the CEO's question "What should I be working on right now?" The answer, discussed throughout this book, is to focus on continually building, strengthening, and systematically aligning the seven essentials that create aligned action. As you read through the previous seven chapters, perhaps you identified one or more essentials that require your attention.

But knowing where to focus is not sufficient. You must also be effective in your actions. How do you actually achieve the alignment? How do you do it?

I would like to focus this last chapter on just one developed skillset, which in my experience is the greatest determinant of your effectiveness. The work of the effective CEO requires a different skillset than you might imagine: mastery in the ability to engage expertise. Creating aligned action requires that you learn *how* to engage experts in coordinated action.

Peter Drucker coined the term "knowledge worker" about 50 years ago. At the time, the economy was still largely an industrial economy based on mass markets of consumers. Now we have gone well beyond an information economy into a conceptual economy. The high growth sectors of the economy are idea driven. The amount of available knowledge is multiplying rapidly.

Identifying and capitalizing on business opportunity requires assembling knowledge into useful innovations, products, and services. As the CEO leading this process, you must master the ability to engage experts from different disciplines. This mastery requires skills as a teacher, coach, and facilitative leader. These skills will help you bring out the best thinking from different perspectives and shape and synthesize these ideas into a coherent plan of action.

WHY ENGAGE EXPERTS?

Consider for a moment the alignment of your car's wheels. When your car is out of alignment, the tires wear unevenly and the steering system is unbalanced. Left unaddressed, your car does not perform at its peak potential and eventually will require costly repairs. To check the alignment, you have to put your car up on a rack and take specific measurements. If the car is out of alignment, the mechanic then makes the adjustments and brings the car into alignment using *physical force.*

By contrast, people do not respond well to mechanical force. When the leader is missing skills in engaging experts, there is often a tendency to revert to command and control tactics. This approach may work in very limited circumstances for a very short time. However, this approach almost never works with knowledge workers over time. People do not perform well in permanent crisis mode. The smartest, most talented people that create the foundations for your success simply will not respond to this approach. They see the permanent crisis as a breakdown of leadership and seek other opportunities.

To create and sustain aligned action over the long term, a different approach is required. While there is not a single right approach, your approach can be much more effective when you consider the nature of expertise and how you lead experts.

By expert, I don't necessarily mean the leading authority in the field, but certainly the leading authority in a particular domain of knowledge with respect to your company. Across all functions of your company, you'll find people – whether in sales, marketing, engineering, operations, finance, information technology, or human resources – who have developed know-how about particular things. Frequently this know-how goes beyond technical knowledge and is embedded in social relationships with customers, suppliers, or fellow employees.

Experts typically identify strongly with their know-how. They value it within themselves as they've built it over a period of many years. Accordingly, they want to be consulted on issues that impact them – and more specifically, on issues where they may be able to contribute. They are not blindly loyal, and will not do what they are told just because you say so. They want to understand why and have a voice in decisions, especially decisions that they will implement. When they actually create the plan with your support, their level of ownership is even greater.

When you master the engagement of experts, not only are you able to create aligned action, you also tap into discretionary effort which accelerates results. When experts are fully engaged, they decide to bring greater effort, energy, and inspiration to their work, above and beyond what is required to simply get by.

HOW TO ENGAGE EXPERTS EFFECTIVELY

Fulfilling your complete definition of success will require the aligned action of individuals from a range of specialties and disciplines, from within and outside of your company. Here are some guidelines for how you can do this most effectively:

1. Learn how to be a coach, teacher, and facilitator. Leading experts is less about what you know or even what any individual knows – but it is about creating a shared field of understanding.

2. Shift your communications model from hub-spoke to a round table. Instead of information flowing from

individuals to you and then back out to other individuals, convene a round table where every expert contributes to the conversation.

3. Teach your experts to teach. Senior leaders in key functions must be adept at communicating their expertise in context. They will know more about their field than their peers – or even you. They must learn how to break this knowledge down so it is digestible and actionable, but not patronizing. Help them appreciate that hoarding information does not make them more valuable. In fact, the opposite is true. When they share and teach in a way that is truly useful, they become more valuable.

4. Focus on desire and opportunity. Before diving into details, make sure you are engaging people's desire to pursue a big opportunity. Ask questions such as "Is what we're thinking about even worth doing? Will it excite and energize us? Sure we could do it, but should we?" When you focus on opportunity, their eyes will light up. Experts want their talents to be deployed in the service of creating – not fixing. Fixing is a temporary state. If you need to fix things, fix them – but then shift to creating.

5. Focus on "what good looks like." Experts love to analyze and criticize. They become adept at seeing problems. Help them to create a vision for what good looks like, so they can teach and operationalize it in

the company. For example, define what a good sales call looks like so people can adopt those principles. Show them how to handle customer situations in the right way. Model great meetings and decisions. When you focus on what good looks like, you get more of it.

6. Focus on "day in the life." Especially in times of rapid change, help people move from conceptual thinking into concrete, operational execution. They know what their day looks like today – what they do, where they spend their time, how things work. Even if they are committed to the future you are articulating, they can't necessarily see how their daily life will change. The faster you help them see this and do it, the more your efforts will stick.

7. Engage experts beyond the four walls of your company. You'll need to draw on expertise in various forms over the life of your company. Some you want to own, some you want to contract for on a more flexible basis. Yet you need these experts to be engaged in your mission just the same – committing discretionary effort to your success.

8. Learn to sift through the smoke and mirrors of expertise and get to results. You must learn who you can trust to deliver results, not simply hide behind technical jargon that makes them sound smart. Powerful agreements on performance are a key tool for you here.

9. Slow down to go fast. Take the time to create a shared understanding of your purpose, customers, and business model. Work out how your key processes will flow and how decisions will be made. As CEO, you are the primary driving force that prevents busyness from creeping into your organization. You must slow people down to ensure effectiveness.

10. Master the principles of adult-learning and group process. When you engage adults in powerful conversations with shared learning, you'll find that innovation and performance improve.

11. Pursue self-mastery. Let go of your need for control or approval. Become a continuously learning expert among experts. Become fully coachable yourself. Hire your own coach. Learn to coach others.

YOUR ROLE AS CEO

Ultimate effectiveness in the work of the CEO requires not only knowing what to focus on, but also mastery in engaging experts. Mastery in engaging experts requires a high level of self-mastery as you grow into a teacher, coach, and facilitative leader. Fortunately, this skillset and mastery can be developed over time.

Just like young King Arthur, no one arrives in the role fully equipped. Focusing on your own development will generate very rapid and sustainable return on effort for you and your company.

RIGHT NOW

"Only three things occur naturally in organizations,
friction, confusion, and underperformance.
Everything else requires leadership."
— PETER DRUCKER

Right now, a sales rep in your company is out on a sales call. Is she communicating in the right way with the customer?

Right now, a product team is deciding what features to include in a new product. Will they make good decisions consistent with your business model?

Right now, your management team is developing a new marketing and sales strategy. Will they think through all of the required pieces to be successful?

Right now, is the right behavior occurring in your company to create sales, profits, growth, and innovation?

Right now, are you focused on the right things as the CEO? Are you doing the true work of the CEO that only you can do?

Do you see the evidence of aligned action that leads to sustainable high performance? If not, where do you need to focus your energy and attention? How will you engage the experts in your company to make it happen?

———————

This book was written to help you answer the question "What should I be working on right now?" Knowing the answer is not enough. Now you must go do it.

Aligned action is not a luxury. It is a requirement for survival, growth and profitability. As CEO, you must work on those essential actions that create aligned action inside your company. Right now.

AN INVITATION

This book is not the final word by any means, but merely the beginning of a conversation. I welcome your comments or questions about the book. I would love to hear stories about what you've learned and how you've applied it. Please send them or call. I promise that I will respond personally.

—————————

To receive an audio companion to this book in mp3 format, please visit www.alignedaction.com/bookaudio.

—————————

To inquire about strategic coaching with Ron Wilder, or to schedule a live, interactive version of this book with you and/or your team, please contact Ron. Ron can be reached by email at ron@alignedaction.com or by phone. To learn more, visit www.alignedaction.com.

ABOUT THE AUTHOR

Ron Wilder serves as a strategic advisor, coach, and teacher to business leaders worldwide. Ron works with CEOs, business owners, executives, entrepreneurs, and experts – in companies ranging in size from one-person start-ups to Fortune 500 corporations.

In 2003, Ron founded Aligned Action, a strategy-focused executive coaching and advisory firm. In Ron's work with clients, he assists leaders in creating big opportunities, taking the seeds of a vision and crafting a strategy to realize it, and aligning the organization to accelerate sales growth and profitability. Ron's work is typically behind-the-scenes, with results occuring *through the leader* who is rapidly developing into a more effective and powerful leader in the process.

Ron's career began in Silicon Valley, where he worked with R.B. Webber & Company, a boutique strategy consultancy and venture capital firm. He held sales, marketing, and corporate development roles for two venture-backed start-ups.

Ron holds a B.S. in Physics from Emory University and an M.S. in Engineering-Economic Systems from Stanford University. He served in the U.S. Naval Reserve and deployed to the Persian Gulf during Operation Desert Storm.

Ron enjoys playing classical piano and is an active practitioner and student of the martial arts. He lives outside of Raleigh, North Carolina with his wife and two daughters.

Ron writes extensively on business and leadership at his blog, found at www.alignedaction.com.